This book belongs
to a girl who always keeps
her dreams in her heart: you.

(your name here)

Believing in dreams is a powerful thing.
Always know that you can reach them!

Also by Ashley Rice

For an Incredible Kid
Girl Power
You Are a Girl Who Totally Rocks

Library of Congress Control Number: 2009902883
ISBN: 978-1-59842-352-5

BLUE MOUNTAIN PRESS is registered in U.S. Patent and Trademark Office.

Certain trademarks are used under license.

Printed in China.
Second printing of this edition: 2010

Blue Mountain Arts, Inc.
P.O. Box 4549, Boulder, Colorado 80306

You Go, Girl...

Keep Dreaming

a special book about
always believing in yourself

updated edition

Ashley Rice

Blue Mountain Press ™
Boulder, Colorado

An Introduction
by Penelope J. Miller

Hi! I'm Penelope J. Miller, and I'm the narrator of this book about reaching your dreams. The very special drawings and writings on these pages were created especially to encourage talented, amazing girls, just like you, to follow their incredible dreams.

Sometimes people don't do the things they really want to do because they're afraid they might mess up. But you should always remember that achieving a real dream actually means a lot of messing up! It's not really messing up at all, though. It's more like practice — like when you're learning to play the piano or ride a surfboard. You may think you haven't got it down quite right at first, but one brilliant and bright day you're suddenly playing a new song or standing up on the surfboard riding a wave. Dreams are that way, too. If you just keep reaching and trying and practicing, one day you'll find yourself in the middle of your own dream come true.

Your dreams are very, very important! They can give you hope and courage in times of change. They can make you braver and bolder and even more amazing than you already are. Dreams mean a lot of things. They mean having the guts to try new adventures and take completely new chances. They mean living and learning and laughing and always reaching further. They mean giving your life everything you've got!

So wherever you are right now and whatever you are doing, I hope you follow your heart, reach the best stars, and always keep on dreaming!

Your friend,
Penelope J.

Believe in yourself and all you want to be. Don't let what other people say or do make you frown. Laugh as much as possible. Let in the good times and get through the bad. Be happy with who and where you are. You are in the right place, and your heart is leading you to a great tomorrow. When circumstances seem difficult, pull through them. This will make you stronger than you think. The longer you practice the habit of working toward your dreams, the easier the journey will become.

You were meant for great things. Learn as much as possible. Always follow your dreams.

Each step you take —
every minute, every day —
is moving you toward
a bright future.
(Don't forget that.)
And you've got
what it takes to be
anything you want to be.

All you've got to do...
is believe in you.

nurse

inventor

artist

businesswoman

friend

chef

astronaut

doctor

princess

president

athlete

scientist

explorer

teacher

writer

architect

dancer

musician

actor

You can be anything!

Girls Who Change the World

There are girls who make things better...
simply by showing up.
There are girls who make things happen,
girls who make their way.
There are girls who make a difference,
girls who make us smile.
There are girls who do not make excuses,
girls who cannot be replaced.
There are girls of wit and wisdom who –
with strength and courage –
make it through.

There are girls who change the world
every day by dreaming and then acting
to accomplish their goals...

girls like you.

You Are a Rainbow in the Sky

You are an
extra-special
somebody.

You are a
special **butterfly**.

You are the
favorite flavor
of the bunch...

like double-
chocolate
cherry pie.

You are
an **angel**,

a joker,

and a **mystery**
that never lies.

Like a dream
sent to the **stars**,
you are...

a **Rainbow** in the sky.

Facts About

YOUR name:

_____

YOUR nicknames:

_____

Three words that describe you:

_____

Bands you listen to most:

_____

YOUR favorite book or movie:

_____

Where you go when you need to go someplace:

_____

Always be **yourself**...
for no one else
can compare to
the **integrity** of
your own
heart.

Helpful Hint #1:
Be True to Your Dreams

Search for friends who value you
for who you are...
not people who want to change you.
Don't be over-influenced by what others do...
even if there are more of them than you.
Never give up the fight to stay true
to your hopes and your dreams...
and the things that mean a whole lot to you.
Even if what you are doing
isn't what everybody else seems to want to do...
always be who you are.
In the end, you'll feel a whole lot better!
And you'll go a whole lot farther.

A Dream Is a Song
That Begins in Your Heart

A dream comes from your
own imagination.
It gives you courage.
It makes you strong.
And it gives you a place
from which to start
making your life the way
you want it to be.
Always believe in
your amazing dreams.

On the Road
of Life...

Be **PROUD** of your hopes, your dReams, and your **accomplishments**. Pursue and achieve goals that mean something to **you**. **Choose** each Road carefully, but allow for whimsy in your life. Sometimes an unexpected **OPPORTUNITY** will lead you someplace exciting and new.

Meet changes head-on and try not to be afraid of them. Be mindful of others' feelings, and take care of your own heart. Keep courage in your back pocket, and you can face anything.

There is **1** rule
you need
to follow as you go
through this world...

If you want to make
your way as a

star...

Do the

best

you can.

Greatness Is...

...a Mountain Scaled in Courage

When the task at hand is a **mountain**
in front of you,
it may seem too haRd to climb.
But you don't have to climb it
all at once —
just one step at a time.
Take one small step...
and one small step...
then **anotheR**...
and you'll find...
the **task** at hand that was a mountain
in front of you...
is a mountain you have climbed.

If you have never **failed**... then you probably have not been "fighting" in the Right "weight" class — with the **best** competition. If you have never been hurt... then you have **PRObably** never gone after **something** you loved. If you have never been **frightened**... then you have probably never put yourself on the line or **cared** about something enough to — **win or lose** — simply give it **everything** you've **got**... you know: give it your all. If you have never **fallen**... then you have not grown or learned how to get up. If you have never **lost**... then you probably have not taken enough **chances**.

So if learning and living involve so much "failing" and faltering... how do you know if you're ever doing anything right?

Because when you fall — you fall, but your heart... it dances.

When the ground falls
out from under you...

...learn to fly.

To Make Your Dreams Real...

You gotta put in the time
and you gotta walk the line
and you gotta keep the sunshine,
the stars, and the ground –
all at once – within your view.
You gotta look for the sublime,
listen to the Road,
and keep your own time...
and you gotta have some fun, too!

Have a blast on the way
to your dreams!

Your Heart Will
Lead the Way

The **best** way to get where you are going
is to follow the compass inside your **heart**.
It's there **right now** — wherever you are —
and it's been there from the start.
On **days** when you may feel a bit
like you've lost your way,
your heart will turn things around.

Keep
GOING
No Matter
What

And if you **trust** in
your own compass,
it will never let you down.

Take These Things with You Wherever You Go...

memories

fun

love

Rai bows

hope

spirit

friendship

courage

a belief in your dreams

a grin in your back pocket

...and a determination
to get you wherever you
need to go.

YOU ARE a
GiRl Who Is...

1. SharP

2. Intelligent

3. Amazing

4. Brave

5. Remarkable

6. Independent

7. Incredible

8. Daring

Write down **3** things
you want to do when you grow up:

1. _____

_____

2. _____

_____

3. _____

_____

Now write down 3 things you want to do this year:

1. _____

_____

2. _____

_____

3. _____

_____

You belong to a long line
of women who began
dreaming as girls
and grew up to be
women of intellect,
courage, vision,
creativity...
women who make
a difference.

And as far as I can tell...

...you are well on your way
   to becoming
   one such woman.

GRowing Up Is HaRd

GRowing up is
not easy to do...

but each time you
grow...

you learn
something new.

And each **time** you
gRow...

you get a little bit
closeR...

to youR dReams
coming tRue.

GRowing up is
not easy to **do**,
but it's woRth it.

How to Make
Your Heart Dance

Find a little **happiness**.
Find a little hope.
Find a little or even a very
   big place where you can go.
Find a little (or big) but very
   excellent dream.
Find some true and some
   Real fun.
If you can **do** these five
   things...

   You've won.

You are an **incredible** girl.

May your heart
always dance.

Helpful Hint #3:
Always Walk in the Sunshine

Whenever you're having a hard time or
you're feeling down or
things aren't going your way...
walk in the sunshine.
It will help you to find
hope for something better.
For there, in the sunshine,
you can best imagine and then act on
your greatest hopes and dreams —
and follow through.
So no matter what you do —
even when clouds surround you —
always walk in the sunshine.

On Hope

You gotta have hope
and you gotta keep trying
and you gotta keep believing
that everything you are striving for
and trying to do is worth something.
You gotta have some heart
and you gotta have drive...
but mostly you gotta have hope...
and hope comes from inside.

What You've Got:

A **graceful** intellect...

a true and **strong** character...

a **brave** sense of wit
and humor and knowingness...

a **respect** for what you **love**...

the guts to go,
reasons to **believe**...

a **unique** ability to face **mountains**...

the agility to **fly**...

...the **heart** to leaRn
and to dReam
and to **walk** a million miles...

a **smile** that can
change things...

...and **style**, Baby, style.

If someone were to write
a **book** about you,
it would be a
book about...

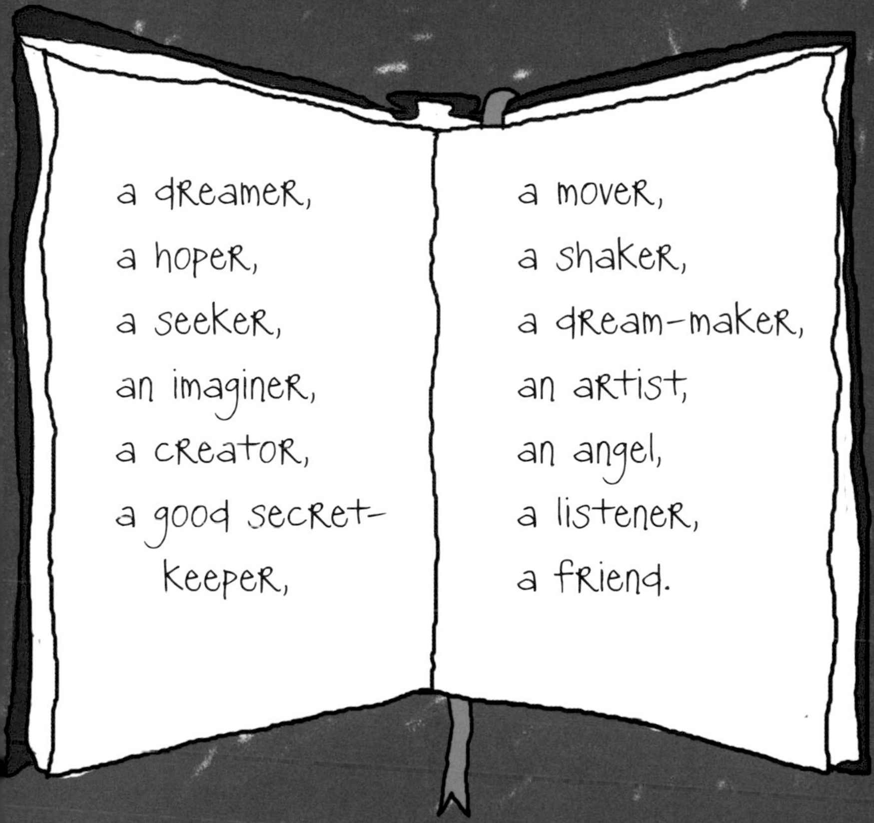

a dreamer,
a hoper,
a seeker,
an imaginer,
a creator,
a good secret-
   keeper,

a mover,
a shaker,
a dream-maker,
an artist,
an angel,
a listener,
a friend.

A girl with a dream
can do anything.
A girl with a **dream**
has got guts.
A girl with a dream
has got moxie.
A girl with a dream –
even if she has something to lose –
will take the **chance** anyway.
A girl with a dream
lives both now
and for tomorrow.
A girl with a dream
never gives up.
A girl with a dream
can do anything.
A girl with a dream
is a girl like **you.**

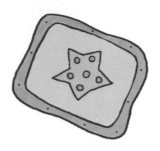

Write down your biggest and brightest
hopes, dreams, and goals...
or anything else you want:

_____

_____

_____

_____

_____

_____

_____

_____

_____

Helpful Hint #4:
Keep Peace in Your Heart

May there always be peace in your heart.
May you find your own pair of wings.
When things seem difficult, turn to your heart.
This is the place you can start imagining...
and dreaming up the life you want to live.
So work hard, with peace in your heart...

...and you'll go far.

You are your own
best adviser,
   your own best judge of
your heart...
   your own best
dream-maker, mapmaker,
   and compass.
You are your own
best go-getter and your
   own best cheerleader
when things are going rough.
   You are you...
      and that's more than
      enough!

You go, girl...
you fly.

How to Get to Your Future:

1. Work hard

2. Study hard

3. Learn as much as you can

4. Invite possibility

5. Don't worry too much

6. Be different

7. Make a plan

8. Lend a hand

9. Laugh

10. Have fun

11. Never give up

12. Make your future
   your own

The Times of our Lives

Sometimes the hardest
times in our lives are
what push us further,
inspire us to be bolder,
teach us about real
hope, dreams, and how
to believe... They help us
to become the greatest
version of that person
we always hoped we'd be...

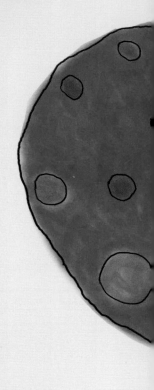

Be proud of all you've
achieved and everything
you are. No matter what
circumstance, state,
or place you may find
yourself in some days,
just keep being you: a
bold, bright star.

YOU are one
of the many gIRls
who aRe

changing

the woRld

foR the betteR.

Keep on dancing.
Keep on trying.
Keep believing,
even after you've been crying.
Keep on daring.
Keep on sharing your heart.
Keep on dreaming...
And always, always,
always, always, always
believe in your dreams.

good things to come

You Go, Girl

Wishing you:
a little peace,
a little **love**,
a little luck,
a little sunshine,
a little **happiness**, and
a little fun.

As far as
Reaching your
dreams and goals...

You can do anything!